Ice and Gaywings

Kenneth Pobo

ISBN 978-0-9866909-4-5

Cover photographs by Sharon Mollerus ("Ice Blues, Lake Superior")
and Dave Bonta ("Fringed Polygala Pair")

Editors: Beth Adams and Dave Bonta
Design: ParcMedia.ca

Published by

qarrtsiluni
www.qarrtsiluni.com

in collaboration with

PHOENICIA PUBLISHING
MONTREAL

www.phoeniciapublishing.com

For Stan

TABLE OF CONTENTS

RIB MOUNTAIN, WISCONSIN

We drive past Rib Mountain,
the highest in a flat state—

sometimes fog mists
its side. Or rain

makes it look like a dark
green ship. Today

the sun, a carpenter,
builds a gold room at the top.

WAUPACA

Sneeze, sit on the porch,
admire night's black leotards
on a line. Irene's
jukebox with "Sugar Shack,"
oh, Waupaca,

we could be happy together
but you refuse me,
the bachelor uncle
you never invite to reunions.

White steeple, white snow
on cornfields. Barn owls

tally up cow misdemeanors.
Cough and sniff

about how life isn't fair anymore,
how strangers should keep to cities

and raise poverty.

A STRETCH OF ROAD BETWEEN SCANDINAVIA AND IOLA

What luck! I remembered to bring
my Herb Alpert CD—any road
is possible when horns

are feisty. If my car breaks down,
goldenrod might mug me. So what?
Here Earth likes to brag up some flower.

Live here? Are you kidding?
I can't give myself completely
to oaks, wind, and fields.

Tomorrow I'll be safe again
behind locks, telling stories
on the phone, spreading lies.

RIVER AND LEAVES

1.

A red doorway of leaves blows open
into a room filled with mourners.
I smell each blackened leaf:
I had forgotten it was September 30th.
His voice must be trapped in the stem
of this red one I put in my pocket.

2.

A few months ago the river was blue-brown.
My friend and I arrived
where lily pads sent white and yellow
blossoms up: floating gazebos. Minnows
tickled the backs of my knees.

The lilies have shriveled into old hands.
Brown water slides toward the city,
bearing acorns. Leaves drop off in wet arms.

3.

I leave the river, pass the junkyard
of apples fallen by the path. River
and leaves: I go to bed.
I hear it is good to mind your dreams.
Mine often smell of soil. I put
the red leaf under my pillow for luck.

Awake. A vase: hours breathe inside.
I can't remember my dream. September
gold flowers fade as they open.

Moon on water. Dark birds
in bright trees. Monarchs head south.
Edges shift and disappear.

CATHERINE TAKEN

Death hides in a corner,
won't come when called.
Waiting to die for decades,
she wears gray dresses,
no pizazz. At 94 she curses
another day of tea
and horehound candy. In her
nursing home bed she looks
surprised, angry—death
sneaks up, cradles her, tries
to make everything all right.

GNATS

Think of people who annoy you.

My neighbors keep
their German Shepherd out 24/7.
My boss fires my friends.
A snotty teller clucks when
I hand her a Canadian check.
Gnats

annoy.
When Stan and I walk in
the June woods, I tap dance,
slap, swat, finger-plug my ears,
rub dead gnats from my eyes.

They surround him. He says
I walk in a "cloud" of gnats.
A high-pitched buzz builds
till I break into

a run back to the cabin
where I wash my hair, black bodies
dotting a white sink—

the silence a relief,
quiet after mass murder.

GAYWINGS

Gaywings bloom in May and into June,
thin blossoms, shorter than an ankle—
they often call as we walk past. Soon
they'll be fading—we'll be back to full-
time jobs. We bend, admire purple fire
burning between a damp maple leaf
and a fern. Looking pale, we're shyer
than they. In a week, they'll come to grief.

THIS MAY

In northern Wisconsin,
we expect to see pink

ladyslippers, but we're early—
they're tardy. We find

their favorite forests
but not a one. It's like expecting

a loveletter from someone
you're nuts about. The postman

brings only junk mail and bills.
Every day. You admit

no letter will come, mope.
Yet you keep looking.

HUMMINGBIRD AND WATER LILIES

In a small restaurant
we drink martinis. My dad
orders for all of us—
is this the fifties? No,

my parents enjoy you.
Back then few families
would laugh with a gay son
and his partner in public.
Some see the past
as a dozen white roses,
blue vase, sunny sill.

My past crashed
into a wall,
no helmet.

As we dig into dinners,
you point us to the window—
a hummingbird flitters
by a feeder,
flies off. You,

a lake that wind gently ripples.
Small waves, early soft
crimson water lilies open.

NORTHERN WISCONSIN

We walk around Shannon Lake
in spring. Everything smells wet,
and lazy afternoon light
makes us feel barely awake
till we pick up our pace, get
up close with flowers, the white
bunchberry, the cinnamon
fern under shade-spotty sun.

This lake lacks a dock, no sign
of people breaking up thin
waves with a horsepowered boat.
Alone: isn't it so fine
to be together here, skin
tingling, no need of a coat?

FALLISON LAKE

June. We search for ladyslippers
growing by pines near boggy ponds.
Wind makes little sound when it stirs—

for now we feel free from dangers,
headlines. The forest's green deepens
June. We search for ladyslippers,

listen to competing songs—birds
belt out their latest number ones.
Wind makes little sound when it stirs

new grass. Take my hand, love. It's yours.
Last autumn's leaves, no longer bronze.
June. We search for ladyslippers

hiding from us interlopers—
when we talk, their silence responds.
Wind makes little sound when it stirs

briefly, a cat who wakes up, purrs,
runs off looking for liaisons.
June. We search for ladyslippers.
Wind makes little sound when it stirs.

EVICTED TURTLES

Where we searched for turtles
became a golf course. A small pond,
now a water trap. Turtles
lolled, paddled around. Messy

and wet, we'd go in
to pull them out,
take them home
till too many died
from air-conditioned rooms. We

learned to let them be, stopped
wading in to grab them, watched
when one would bloop
or another stick its weird head out
to see if we were worth looking at

before water's dark door opened
to let them in.

MINNOWS UNDER THE BOAT

While rowing through lilypads
to a reedy sandbar,
a tongue sticking out,

I see minnows zigzag,
slipping away quickly,
like an owl's hoot

when I lie in a rented bed,
the moon thumbing me
like magazine pages.

SANDBAR

In a fiberglass tub,
a dead fish and grass smell
lead to a knifeline of sand
scratched on the bay. Summers

I crave stagnation,
dragonflies, reeds
and sunning turtles.

I pull in, tie the anchor
to a stump. An oriole skims
yellow water lilies.
A fisherman sings,

his bullfrog voice
in weedy water.

An intruder, I row out.

HERON

A blue heron raises
her weapon beak—

with gray-blue wings and
Mozart-writing-a-scherzo eyes,
we don't dare get

too close. She demands
distance, can snag a snake,
eat every bit.

LOONS

How many years have we come here?
Forty for me, for you, seven.
We've never seen loons swim so near,

almost to where we stand by clear
lake water. You: "This is heaven!"
How many years have we come here

looking for wildlife, even deer,
eating gardens back home, but then
we've never seen loons swim so near,

dipping, diving, showing no fear
as we try to be quiet men.
How many years have we come here

to escape the rest of the year,
to touch without job-stress again?
We've never seen loons swim so near,

yet they keep alert—they know we're
close. Will they fly? We don't know when.
How many years have we come here?
We've never seen loons swim so near.

IN THE WILDLIFE CENTER

Through the screen door
of their cage, we stare in—
both owls stare back,
make no sound:

pollen falling gently
on birch branches
in depths of a forest.

TAMARACK SWAMP

A wooden path gets us
close to a pitcher
plant colony. I leave planks
to drop my eyes
into the biggest one. You stay

on the path, snap pictures.
I had forgotten spongy
sphagnum moss, crash
right through. Wet socks,

shins. I look at you,
a few steps ahead,
wonder what I'm not seeing,
what dangers hide. Silent,

we keep walking.

MINOQUA

Taxidermy, resorts, gift shops,
restaurants, Minoqua
fills with families and

fishermen. In fall, the town's
like a party with a few
guests left till hunting season.

February fishermen cut holes
in ice. April's warmer
winds ruffle a wildflower

blanket, streets runny
with the thawing blood
of winter's corpse.

UP NORTH

Up north we sit in Someplace Else:
my friend, the only woman
except for waitresses.
Orange jackets, hunters
talk of last year's kill, Eagle River's
upcoming Snowmobile Championship.

A portrait of a deer in the woods
with a woman's face
hangs above us. Forks, knives,
coffee cups, and painted hooves
fleeing through lichen.

At the bar a drunk swerves
between whiskey and peanuts,
trips out to his car, a deer on its top.
His wife, probably at home,
a wedding picture above the bed:
she in white, he in black.
Orange sky pursuing whatever moves.

VERN BARNINGHAM

A lighthouse keeper,
he times Lake Superior's
lights, keeps lenses turning
so skippers can tell

islands apart. Up high,
silent, he watches
lake birds, wave tips.
Many keepers prefer

the slap of water
against shore, seasons
like four strange voices
in trees. Storms can't

quite cover the beam.
Vern makes light
the way farmers coax
earth into harvest.

OFF LAKE SUPERIOR

Many sank here, names
lost. Men trusted a boat—

clouds, purple welts,
rose off the bow:

water's dictionary
left out "mercy"—

closed eyes,
an open mouth.

THE MANISTEE

1.

1883. For five days
we hoped the storm that chained
us to Bayfield would free us—

Lake Superior, a man
dancing alone, knows every move,
yet who could guess his calm

when killing? Sun out,
we left, risking water's
iron hooks. Waves

grew higher as we went farther
out, beyond the light,
where we remembered land

like childhood. Any other life,
dead letters and promises.
When the ship cracked

open, wind carried no messages,
our bodies lost. Our families
built absence a home.

2.

1884. Fishermen find a silver spoon
engraved with "Manistee"
in a trout's belly.

SUPERIOR'S GHOSTS

We drink milkshakes in Bayfield,
45s line walls. Tourists
scrape off jobs, amble

into shops. Lake Superior
has devoured many sailors,
holds secrets. A ghost

sits at any table. Someone
who died in the 1890s
pulls up a chair, sees

our Tommy Hilfiger shirts,
digital watches. Yet his lake
is also ours—icy water,

stunned moon. You and I talk
about tomorrow. He already
knows what he'll do—stop by

a restaurant, listen, walk
on sand, watch for his body
between iron-scented waves.

TOM KESSLER, STOCKTON ISLAND, 1887

No one back in Louisville asks
if I'm happy. They pity me,
alone, long winters, no family.

Logging. We scratch ourselves raw
from mosquitoes. Saws cut off
fingers, limbs. Many pack up
for warmer places,
not a city of hardwoods.

Stockton Island surrenders
fall and spring quickly. Winter
ice turns shores jagged.
If I had a son, would I
tell him to try this work?
He'd have to like hearing
wind in trees, smelling peat,

wood smoke, oxen. The company's
hitting hard times, men
laid off and fired. Maybe
I'm next. What to do
when I leave? I'm full

of trees, birds, the coming
of spring when Superior thaws.

SUSPENSION BRIDGE

We slap and slap
black flies. I remove
rust-reddened sneakers.
You snap

pictures. Water bruises
our feet: we walk on
cold sky, roomy,
imagine miners who worked

in towns that sprawled
and fell,
head off in

different directions.
Later I warm
swollen feet
as you drive us
to a river
cutting into the Lake.

We walk over
a suspension bridge—

how familiar,
you and I on
a trembling bridge,
death flowing
beneath us,

Superior's purple star
calling us to come
get it.

Acknowledgments

Thanks to the editors of the following journals, where some of these poems, occasionally in slightly different form, first appeared:

"Rib Mt" *Dogwood Journal* 2005
"Waupaca" *Grain* 1992
"A Stretch" *Wisconsin academy review* 1989
"River And" *Folio* 1987-88
"Catherine" *Moonwort Review* 2005
"Gnats" *Native West Press* 2003
"Gay Wings" *Brittle Star* 2004
"This May" *Sea Change* 2003
"Hummingbirds And" *modern words* 2004
"Northern Wis" *One Trick Pony* 2002
"Fallison" *Tipton Poetry Journal* 2006
"Evicted Turtles" *Pudding House Press* (forthcoming)
"Minnows Under" *Midwest Quarterly* 1989
"Sandbar" *Orbis* 1991
"Heron" *Blue Unicorn* (forthcoming)
"Loons" *Main Channel Voices* 2005
"Tamarack Swamp" *Kansas City Star*
"Up North" *Island* 1985
"Vern B" *Porcupine* 2001
"Off Lake Sup" *Orbis* 1991
"The Manistee" *Porcupine* 2001
"Superior's Ghosts" *Heartlands* 2003
"Tom Kessler" *Philadelphia Poets* 2003
"Suspension Bridge" *Spoon River Quarterly* 1997

A note on the award

Ice and Gaywings, by Kenneth Pobo, was the first-place winner of the 2011 *qarrtsiluni* poetry chapbook contest, selected by Luisa Igloria.

Ice and Gaywings was simultaneously published in electronic form at http://iceandgaywings.com, as a downloadable audio file; and in this print edition, available through the publisher's website, www.phoeniciapublishing.com, and Amazon.com.

About the author

Kenneth Pobo has four full-length collections of poetry and, including *Ice And Gaywings*, twenty chapbooks. He began writing at age fifteen. He teaches creative writing and English at Widener University in Chester, Pennsylvania. He and his partner and two cats enjoy gardening, music, and the Wisconsin Northwoods. You can catch Ken's radio show, Obscure Oldies, on Saturdays from 6-8:30pm EST at wdnrfm.org.